W9-COT-201

spot

AFRICAN ANIMALS

CROCODILES

by Mary Ellen Klukow

AMICUS | AMICUS INK

foot

tail

Look for these words and pictures as you read.

scutes

jaw

Is that a log?

No!

It's a crocodile!

Crocs live in the water.

They lie in the sun to warm up.

Look at the scutes.
They are bony scales.
They are hard.

scutes

Look at the tail. Swish!
The crocodile uses it to swim.

tail

jaw

Look at the jaw.
Crocs can't chew.
But their bite is strong.
Prey can't escape.

Look at the foot.
It has three claws.
It can dig a nest.

foot

Parents carry the
babies to the water.
They carry them in their mouth.

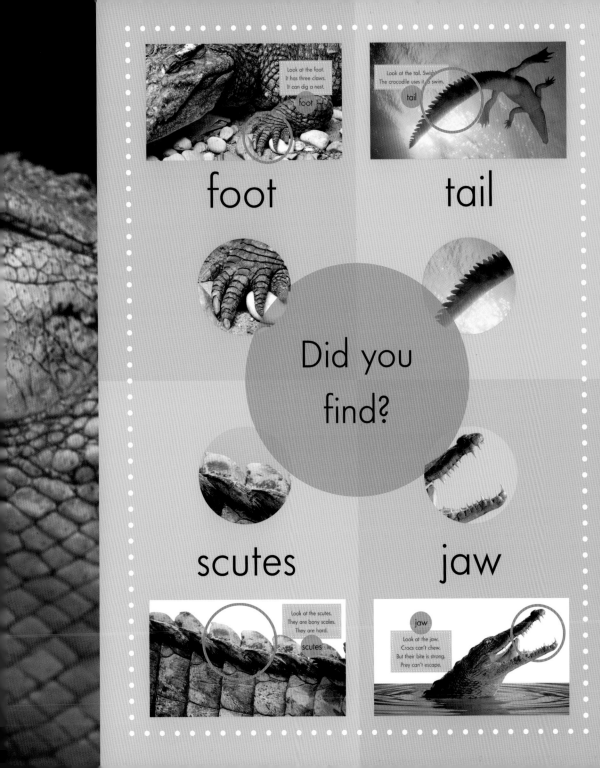

Look at the foot.
It has three claws.
It can dig a nest.
foot

foot

Look at the tail. Swish!
The crocodile uses it to swim.
tail

tail

Did you find?

scutes

Look at the scutes.
They are bony scales.
They are hard.
scutes

jaw

jaw

Look at the jaw.
Crocs can't chew.
But their bite is strong.
Prey can't escape.

Spot is published by Amicus and Amicus Ink
P.O. Box 1329, Mankato, MN 56002
www.amicuspublishing.us

Library of Congress Cataloging-in-Publication Data
Names: Klukow, Mary Ellen, author.
Title: Crocodiles / by Mary Ellen Klukow.
Description: Mankato, Minnesota : Amicus, [2020] |
  Series: Spot. African animals | Audience: K to Grade 3.
Identifiers: LCCN 2018025775 (print) | LCCN
  2018031248 (ebook) | ISBN 9781681517193 (pdf) |
  ISBN 9781681516370 (library binding) |
  ISBN 9781681524238 (paperback)
Subjects: LCSH: Crocodiles--Africa--Juvenile literature.
Classification: LCC QL666.C925 (ebook) | LCC QL666
  C925 K58 2020 (print) | DDC 597.98/2--dc23
LC record available at https://lccn.loc.gov/2018025775

Printed in China

HC 10 9 8 7 6 5 4 3 2 1
PB 10 9 8 7 6 5 4 3 2 1

Wendy Dieker and Alissa Thielges, editors
Deb Miner, series designer
Ciara Beitlich, book designer
Holly Young, photo researcher

Photos by iStock/vusta cover, 16; iStock/
tomodaji 1; Alamy/Colin Marshall, 3;
Dreamstime/Arno Meintjes 4-5; Getty/
Jason Edwards 6-7; Getty/Mark Deeble
and Victoria Stone 8-9; iStock/johan63
10-11; 123RF/sasilsolutions 12-13; Age
Fotostock/Roger De La Harpe 14

CROCODILES